Two Essays

*

Traumear

*

Two Essays

1 What it Means to be a Human Being   pg 1

2 Human Beings: Creatures and Gods   pg 34

*

*

These two essays were originally written in German, along with twenty others on similar topics, in 1994, by the author and then translated by him into English in 2018. They contain much fundamental thought that is explored and expanded in other, longer essays. At times the reader may do well to keep in mind that creative thought is not as readily translated as, say, a story or a novel, because in the case of the former the language itself is depended upon to supply its store of vernacular truth, as during the creation of such research essays, which are more like artworks than like conceptual constructs.

*

What it means to be a Human Being

All sinks away beneath me and I stand upon a foundation that bears up only me. Here I am secure, albeit alone. Mind you, I am active and capable of change. Strength streams into me and I realize myself in terms of action. My work lies before me and it grows.

I define myself as a human being because I know that this strength streams into me. It is a human attribute to be able to know this. Whoever does not know this will time and again behave inhumanly. I do not mean any particular strength but just strength. It streams into me because I have decided to work. My intention here is not to define philosophically but to philosophize in human fashion. Whoever resents me for this can always read something else. I know that what is in me to write down just now is useful for me and also for others. For that reason I write it down. I draw my own benefit from this while I write. I would not be able to write it if I did not have the benefit for others in mind. With regard to the benefit of human work, one's own benefit is not to be separated from that for others. We do well to keep that in mind.

*

Strength:

Actually it should suffice simply to know *of* this strength. When I say that it streams into me, then that sounds as if that strength also existed outside of me. However it cannot be called strength until it appears within me. I wonder does anything at all exist outside of me that I then call strength when it appears within me? And why exactly do I refer to it as a 'streaming into me'? Here is the strength and I know of it, and I also know that I myself have not produced it. This may

1

well be what is most important about this business, that I have the use of this strength while I do not forget that I am not myself that strength. Whoever supposes he himself is this strength hands himself over to magic and gets involved with wizardry in this way, and to that extent and degree he forfeits his humanity.

If I were this strength it would depend on me. However it does not depend on me. Neither do I depend on it – only inasmuch as I wish to be a human being. As a human being I declare myself as dependent on this strength and this dependence can be individual or personal. In both cases I am not only a human being but also free. How do I arrive at this freedom? This strength, by dint of its being human, frees me from all that is not human. And this is what we mean by human freedom, namely to be free of all that is not human.

Now how do I declare myself dependent upon this strength, and what am I when I am not yet a human being and free? This does not interest us in this work, because we want to limit ourselves entirely to that which is human, and which is free or desires to be free. People as such, who do not want to be free and are happy in their dependence upon one another and on their circumstances shall occupy us another time. They do not want to know this human strength and somehow they manage otherwise.

This strength I mean is human and yet we are not this strength. It is greater than we are until we are entirely free, and entirely human, and then we are equally great with it and manage with it, even as I at this moment manage with it. If now we want to be freed from what is not human, we may prepare ourselves for this strength and for its prospective influence. This preparation is *virtuous*. What we, with right, call virtue is preparation for the influence of this human, humanizing strength. And all our virtue relates and extends to others. I cannot be virtuous in myself, or in relation to myself. There can be no virtuous individual.

*

Virtue:

Virtue prepares us for the coming human strength. It is the essence of virtue to mediate between human beings who want to be free, and whoever is virtuous will be free. I may ask myself now how I should behave and respond in your presence and in the presence of others in order to approach this liberating human strength. Virtue consists of response and behaviour. In the presence of what is not human I behave, in this or that way, and in the company of human beings I respond.

Now before we get caught up in mere concepts, we should really imagine virtue as principally a courageous striving outward from our inhibited state of being and from our limiting relationships into a worthy[1] existence. We are in fact inhibited inasmuch as we suppose we have to stick to our usual way of being, and of behaving as others supposedly bid and forbid us. Our inhibition persists until we are so tired of merely existing that death seems to us a liberation. In our relationships we may be like prisoners, like slaves whose master never appears. All they undertake relates to nothing that might in truth support or strengthen them. A relation between me and you, for example, should at the same time stand open to others, so that at any time we may extend our existence and augment our flexibility. Without such an open acceptance of our fellow human beings, relationships are blind and they inhibit us; they are liable to turn into calamities, which then have to yield to force, if they do not undermine themselves.

---

[1] I translate *würdig* as worthy

3

Virtue then implies such behaviour and conduct that allows us to escape from our blind conditioning and from our slavish inhibitions – into a worthy existence. We have some notion of such an existence even while we half consciously still curse the day of our birth. Although the less we try to imagine such a worthiness the better, all the same, some kind of comparison is bound to be available to us at the time, or else we would not appear to ourselves like unpopulated spaces and dates that never arrive. A virtuous human being is in any case courageous in that even in his run-down or degenerate state he is still able to surmise that a worthy existence is possible. The possibility of being worthy means more to him than that his feeling of being unworthy should come to an end. He imagines this worthiness perhaps as something that will endow him with value and the world with meaning. He would never be able to bear being a worthless human being in a meaningless world, so he has painted the future on earth as remarkable and as accessible to reason and understanding. What lies ahead of him should first dissolve into nothing, so he supposes, in order then to prove itself as appreciable and objective.

He promises himself almost everything on the basis of his being brave. The positive quality of his future conduct and behaviour he imagines as concealed in this stalwartness. "I want to be brave," he says, "no matter how unpredictably I apply myself or how problematical I seem to myself, or how much everything I come across nauseates me." Being brave means persevering until he sees sense, until reason emerges again. Courage allows him to proceed in the direction of reason without actually depending on it. He cares little for his reputation as long as he can avoid pettiness, conceit and getting bogged down in the past when it is too late to do anything about it. Courage, in other words, is its own reward just so long as he keeps it up, no matter what happens or does not happen. He does not hold out for a time, but always and for all time, so that something new surprises him only because he did not expect it.

*

A worthy existence:

Even though the brave and courageous one can imagine a worthy existence, he does not trust himself to approach it, because he knows it cannot come when he expects it to come. For that reason too, the courage he means is its own reward. A worthy existence cannot be earned. While he does not earn it and cannot understand it, he has a notion of it as of a mystery. This mystery of a worthy existence has revealed itself to him and it would not occur to him to try to manipulate it with his bare intellect. He knows it as a revealed good to which freedom attaches.

However he also meets some who lead a worthy existence. Perhaps he comes across them in books, listens to their symphonies, participates in their conversations. This uplifts and fortifies him then; it makes him think and draws his attention. Not that he wants to exist like they, but he wishes to be worthy like they. So again, he does not imitate but he allows himself, by this existence as a mystery, to be – ennobled.

The brave one is ennobled by the mystery of worthy existence. He feels this and senses it, and this is why he allows himself to be moved and motivated as much as possible by this mystery. Always and often he keeps it within sight – as mystery. This accounts for his prowess and adeptness. These, along with courage, are implied by virtue. More of that later.

*

Whoever exists worthily thinks of his existence as duty and privilege. In order to exist more worthily he will care for

5

the one who is not yet worthy. In this consists his dignity, which grows organically. Such as he is, here and now – this he knows – so others also want to be, or so they would wish to be if they knew and understood what it means and what a difference it makes – to be worthy. He is a carrier of this mystery and he is familiar with it and he could not be other than helpful to others who might become equally familiar. Not he himself – this he understands – but his dignity motivates others to a virtuous longing for a worthy existence. His straightforward, uncomplicated existence, which remains open to all sides for development, unfolds in others as the wish to set out upon such a development. He notices this and offers support. Virtue has to be learned, and this takes time. He of course has means at his disposal of which the other one has no knowledge and of which he cannot have knowledge until he has proved himself as virtuous. So he offers his aid. Capable and brave the other one should become, so that he will then be able to take advantage of good strength, to make use of it. Prematurely this strength cannot possibly come to him. If he has not at all bothered with it, he will fare like all people who tend to avoid what is human. Finally then humanity, that which is human, has to insist on itself ruthlessly, and such an experience can be hellishly painful. The human being who stands by and cannot help has to wait until the catastrophe has played out to its end. And in this way, time and again, is humanity betrayed into the hands of the people. Never again should that be necessary and yet it happens. How does it happen that still nowadays people find themselves in the position where they violate what is truly human? One can only imagine that this is somehow connected with a compromising attempt at assimilation by human beings who want to be recognized even by people. They do not want to appear different from them – so as not to be liked and not persecuted by them. However that is exactly what happens then, if not outwardly then inwardly.

Whoever has a notion at all of a worthy existence does well not to try to avoid the responsibility that is a necessary part of it, especially not in some popular environment, since people have no familiarity with it.

*

The responsibility of the one who is worthy:

Being worthy makes us responsible. In the presence of people we have to be in the clear about that, which means we must not pretend that we are not different and also we must not act as if we had achieved or earned worthiness. While achievement and merit play a role (it would be wrong to pretend otherwise) the quality of being worthy, which is what this is about in the end, is and remains a gift. What we do have to earn, in a most particular sense, is our clear vision, so that we recognize the gift for what it is and so that we do not mistake it for a 'might'[1] or for a command. And what we may achieve, also in a particular sense, is, so to speak, any room we make in ourselves for this gift, so that we ourselves also have the benefit of it, rather than merely knowing about it and standing hungry and thirsty while others eat. So, to be sure, without achievement and merit we cannot get on, because soon we would mistake this quality of being worthy; or we might become unaccepting and unreliable. All the same, all the achieving and deserving comes to nothing when our main concern is not that which is worthy and which ennobles our existence.

---

[1] I translate *Macht* as might, which is not the same as power. Power is ethical, while might is not ethical but arbitrary.

7

No difference exists then between me and my existence. As I am, so I am here and now.[1] People do not understand me because they cannot, not because they do not want to or do not try hard enough. I would be silly to worry about that. They cannot understand me, nor my achievements, nor my merit, since these do not become understandable except by engagement with what is worthy, which is a gift. I am responsible for what is worthy, not for people's understanding of it. I am not responsible for those who cannot possibly know anything of, or about, worthiness. And if someone can now understand when previously he could not, then I congratulate him. Now I can help him to be competent and brave, which is to say virtuous, and he can help me in the same way – while I myself, or my abilities and merits, neither were nor are the origin of the worthiness which nourishes him now.

I am responsible for worthiness, not for, or to, people. The popular assimilation, for me, is tantamount to – betrayal. As soon as I try to persuade people that really I am the same as they, I am setting myself up for being 'cursed'. It appears to me then that people are 'cursing' me; in reality worthiness has to withdraw from me, and this I experience as persecution. So any wish to escape from people is misguided; I might just as well remain among them. That worthiness flees from me, that is what should concern me, and in view of that I may right away call to mind my true good fortune – namely that I am different and that I know what it means to be worthy.

I recall to mind who I am and that I am fortunate and this, time and again, implies my responsibility.

*

---

[1] ' Being here and now' is, I believe, the best translation of the German 'Dasein', even though I often translate it as existence. Shall we assume that in order to exist properly we have to be here and now?

8

That I am different, and that I am different here and now – let me not try to conceal this from people, who know nothing of worthiness. Hypocrisy is a betrayal of what is worthy and the curse is not long in arriving. The more I become assimilated to people, the further away from me worthiness has to flee, and I experience this as persecution precisely because I have, in the past, experienced worthiness myself. So it is important for me that in the presence of people I stay alert and practice awareness, in other words that I know what it means to be unworthy, while my recognition of it is not judgmental. Why should I stay away from people? What nonsense! It would bring me nothing. The possibility of betrayal is always in me, in my thinking and feeling, in my habits and customs. Distancing myself from people might at most change my problems. So for example it might, for a time, be more suitable for me to work from my inner being rather than in line with my outer being. The work is essentially the same. And the curse can have its effect in either direction. If the spirit of worthiness needs to distance itself from me, I will feel the pain as readily within as without me. Whether I see the presumed enemy within or without, I am equally cursed. So self-hatred is only superficially, not essentially, different from the hatred of people. And whoever would persuade us that we hate ourselves because people hate us, he is guilty of irresponsibility and of unworthiness. Just as silly would be the opposite interpretation, that we hate people because we hate ourselves.

The irresponsible assimilation works the curse, which turns into hatred. In reality self-hatred and people-hatred never appear independently from each other, as one might expect, because once we have experienced worthiness, our inner being and our outer being are joined and may be experienced by us at ease in reality as inward or outward being. The separateness of inner from outer being is called damnation. To be damned means that for that time I neither know the outward nor the inward, for both are in reality one. I unconsciously stray back and forth between the inner and outer, mostly unaware that there is a difference. I am unconsciously pushed back and forth between the two, like destiny's toy, unacceptable to and unaccepting of the worthy gift.

If now I appear before people as one who has achieved and earned the worthy gift, I am really saying to them that no such gift exists in reality.

I should be proud of the fact that worthiness is gifted to me. However it is a human-natural, not an arrogant, pride that will not allow me to compare myself to people. After all they know or understand nothing of human worthiness. Why did I in the beginning behave virtuously? Only because I had a notion of human worthiness. The strength that revealed itself to me – I did not choose it so that anyone might admire me for it. If I am in danger of arrogance, let me be humble, so that I remain responsible for the worthiness and do not have to become responsible for myself, which never turns out well.

In what sense now am I responsible for this human worthiness? It rests upon me as a burden, so that I will bear it in the presence of human beings. It is gifted to me so that I pass the gift on in my works and consequently possess it in reality myself.

However still more important is the following: This human worthiness is the actual proof that I am a human being, and anyone who has dealings with me is bound to be touched by it, whether he is conscious of it or not. Every such contact is meaningful and valuable. I do good by being worthy here and now – and I am worthy so long as I am willing to honour in justice all unpredictable and imponderable reactions.

Human worthiness is therefore principally responsible in that it does not merely work and then draw back but that, beyond the work-effect, it incorporates the reaction to it.

For that reason one speaks of human worthiness as of creative potential. We make ourselves responsible for the effect of this worthiness. We honour every reaction to our human being-here-and-now, and we do that with as much justice as possible. This means that every such reaction is considered with a view to its own basis, if such a basis exists, and not categorically.

So if we consider ourselves to be a member of a group and have rehearsed the various criteria that mark us as a member of that group, and then, upon feeling challenged, we reacts evasively with phrases and formulas and principles, we behave neither worthily nor as a human being. However we are not faced by such challenges unless we already posses a degree of human worthiness, so even on account of that are such challenges meaningful for us. And then we find in them always again the precise opportunity for the embodiment of our worthiness, and it should matter to us that we deal with such challenges responsibly – which means responding justly to every challenge, and not categorically. Of course it happens that we ignore such a challenge. The next one perhaps we recognize, however not thoroughly. The third time we finally engage. Now we do not valuate in one way or another on the basis of some previously made judgment, but in line with the concrete occasion and the unique instance.

The one who is worthy here and now is aware that he is being effective whether the effect is recognized or not; and he knows that it is a good effect whether or not anyone thanks him for it; and he remains worthy here and now – let us for a change put it like this – no matter what the reaction and even if there is no reaction to his effect, so that in this way he is making himself responsible.

*

Awareness[1] and damnation:

As human beings, among people, we do well to remain aware: so that we do not assimilate ourselves and so that we do not withdraw from them but respect them.

As people we are 'dammed' inasmuch as we do not acknowledge real strength and consequently we know nothing of human worth. Also we are not virtuous, not courageous and competent. And that does not bother us at all, that we are dammed, because only from the human point of view is that a disadvantage. The Dam keeps us so thoroughly back and away from anything human that we have no notion whatsoever of what exists on the other side of it. For that reason too we do not think of it as a dam but simply as a limit set to our

---

[1]Now not everyone will be happy with the various words I use to translate the German word 'Besinnung', which can mean consciousness, consideration, reflection. What is telling about the word, and especially apt for our purpose here, is its reflexive aspect. The German will say: Ich besinne mich, which describes something he does to himself. One cannot 'besinnen' something, only oneself. The closest English equivalent to 'besinnen' I can find is: to 'bethink' oneself. Mind you, unlike the German 'besinnen', one can allegedly bethink one's troubles etc., in the sense of dwelling with one's thought on them. Again, this is not possible with 'besinnen'. I avoid the awkwardness of the lack of a sure single-word translation by using several terms and I hope that the context will do the rest. Also I should mention that when a German says: 'Ich besinne mich,' he might simply mean: I am reflecting, or recalling something. By comparison, to be truly aware, in English, we must take advantage of the community of our senses. What counts is that in the German text the verb 'besinnen' refers to a crucial turning to our inward being in response to an inward urgency or challenge.

12

knowing and understanding. We do have a notion of something like a breakthrough, however this would lead to what is negative, deadly and evil, which we find interesting, positive and fascinating. As people, being dammed, we 'live', so to speak, backwards; or we remain standing, being self-satisfied.

If it happens now that this good strength of which we as people know nothing rises up in us or reaches into us, or if it influences us from outside in such a way that we are momentarily horrified, as if out of our mind or 'beyond ourselves', then we have the opportunity to become aware. The occasion offers.

From the popular standpoint, the way we as people see it, these two incentives to awareness are possible. Human beings, we have said, cannot relate to us if we are 'damned'. They would like to value and appreciate us as people who are somehow motivated to be sensible and aware. They hold themselves responsible for that. From the point of view of human beings, only one real motivation exists, because for them inside and outside are connected, as within and without, and both amount to a single whole reality. They view themselves as whole, whereas we, for the first time now, notice, since we have been stimulated to awareness, on what shaky ground we have stood. Not only do we notice for the first time that for us there is such a possibility as a connected inward and outward being but right away it also becomes unpleasantly evident to us that these two existential possibilities only exist for us separately, as inside and outside.[1]

As a result then the continuation of our previous, unaware reverse-life is no longer possible for us. In the Hebrew culture this is imagined as two strong angels at the portal of

---

[1] So for example as psyche and this world, or as material nature and supernature.

13

paradise who prevent those, who have been chucked out, from returning. In the realm of folk-history however the separation between the popular and the human realm is not yet so complete as at the present time, when human beings happily can turn towards people and respect them in their own right.

From our human point of view it is now possible to appreciate the concept of 'folk', because that which was gradually loosened and eased away stands separately judged now, so that human beings, who themselves have meanwhile come to maturity, are now able to turn towards people with an honourable regard.

*

People who have experienced this stimulation to become aware, right away have the possibility to enter upon relations with human beings but first they must actually practice real awareness. The stimulation itself does not suffice. This is understandable, because those who have become aware of the two sides of their 'bipolar' existence and cannot yet see a connection are in bad shape indeed. They experience the extremity of guilt and an immense tedium; a horrifying emptiness yawns beneath them.

"Come to your senses now, you human being!" one says to such a one, and one uses the word 'human being', setting it in front of the afflicted one as a goal. "If you really want to become a human being, come to your senses now, practice awareness! *Bethink yourself.*" One encourages him, because one knows full well that he himself must now respond to that new stimulation. For example this state of being stimulated in that existential manner may manifest itself as extreme nervousness in someone. Then, to be sure, this 'state of nerves' is to turn into awareness for him. It is to become instrumental for him as he shapes his awareness. Or let us say this initial stimulation is this time an anxiety. Then let him be anxious to become aware. Or he gets into a rage. Ire, rage, fury surprise him. Right away let us help him come to peace and rest in his new awareness – not so that he will no longer be in a rage, or nervous, or anxious, this is very important, but so that he will become more human. We can all become more human, we will never get to an end. The beginning however is difficult, because this awareness is in fact something totally new. It always presupposes a degree of self-overcoming.

At one time I was virtually damned and I was told to be hard on myself. I should categorically join the ranks of the dead – violate myself, the way those who are damned behave in the realm of the dead. I even did that for a while. I was praised for that and rewarded. I was sometimes better at it than the dead and I found it dammed easy to excel at their one-sided disciplines. Then, thank God, I was stimulated to become aware and in my case that showed up as half a mental disturbance – it was up to me to supply the other half, intentionally. First the awareness came to me and then I came to it. In order to come to awareness I had to overcome my unproductive self. I did that then too. Overcoming my self was something quite different from doing violence to myself – as in my youth and especially during my teens it had been preached to me. In those days I was supposed to force myself into a social category. I succeeded in that too, but violence and force were barely necessary, one only had to abide by the social norms and learn the popular sign-language of the people, who after all knew everything that there was to know. However once the overcoming of self began, any amount of self-discipline was child's play in comparison because now it made sense and had meaning. From now on human being was a notion I cherished as my goal. None of any of this had I imagined as it turned out.

Actually the so-called self, or ego, does not exist until it arises in reaction to that awareness of the senses and in contradiction to it. First one hates, then one can love. First one curses, then one can bless. First one is damned, then one can become human. During this lengthy resurrection one is involved in a meaningful process.

Come to your senses. Begin with that, when mental disturbances afflict you, when the psyche does not leave you in peace, when mania undermines you and when depression falls on you. That infernal tiredness and lethargy, the madly exciting energy, the discouraging melancholy, the unreasonable self-hatred: those are all invitations to the dance of true sensibility. You step out of the damnation and into that sensibility, that reflection and that contemplation – all forms of awareness. Whoever dares overcomes himself.

*

The comparison of damnation and awareness is reasonable not because the damned one can readily come to his senses and to awareness, which after all is not the case, but because a sensible human being, due to his presence of mind, is able to reach a helping hand to the damned one – in case he would accept it. The very secret of the human race in any case lies hidden in human awareness. We do not merely pretend this is so; it really is so. Whoever learns to be aware and practices awareness and does nothing else – he automatically becomes aware of his human-racial origin. That, after all, is where we all started. Why not remain with this topic for a while. The traditional mythology and the Darwinism we leave to one side for the moment. We will say a few words about our biological/organic origin. Something is fidgeting in the archetypal slime and only a few – and they rarely – have seen fit to comment on it. Equally we can do without the monad and with any attempt to accompany it during those first creative experiments of the human race – because here and now, today, at this moment, we have the opportunity to engage awarely with all that is truly traditional. Perhaps one should mention that in accordance with this affinity, this binding relation, all difference between the future and the past disappears.

Those who are frightened by this are on the right path. Let them courageously, not with half a heart, head off in this direction. Our origin as human destiny then looks different for each of us and we should make our peace with that. My own personal sensibility may well be aware to the reader here. Right away, as soon as know that, I create similar possibilities for the reader in that way.

Reflect right now, as only you can and wish, on your human destiny and know how in this way you make possible powerful connections between things that have long departed and for good reason. Know that you cannot let these things depart until you have cleverly managed that destined connection between them. We cannot let go of things until they are separated from us. Previously our involvement with them was indifferent, they were name- and numberless, massive or simply – loose. We have no desire to make a mystery out of it since it already is one. Whatever is loose is to be bound. Awareness and origin become one as destined unification. Possibilities of procreation and regeneration, that have barely been imagined until now and by only a few, exist for us human beings. Can a human being imagine a more noble goal than that a damned one should come to his senses and to his body of knowledge?

*

Very likely 'Besinnung' is too simple a word for many who promise themselves more from meditation and contemplation. However we can manage with it. We 'bethink ourselves' until a door opens in front of us and then we enter. Some kick the door in and fall into the room with it, which

17

defeats the purpose. The one who meditates (let us use that word for a while) knows that the door opens even as he knocks, and knowing this makes all the difference. The damned one knows of no door and he does not knock. When he says that he reflects (*daß er sich besinnt*) he is reflecting on something he has imagined or on something he has represented to himself, and so he always only discovers – himself. Over a period of time this is, of course, deadening. Instead of making connections, he disconnects himself. Every human being has the power to loose and to bind, but the damned one will not play along – unless he does it nevertheless, and then there is great joy.

Origin and destiny – how is that conceivable? We will succeed with the concept 'humanity'. This allows us to get hold of a before and an after the condition of being damned. After all, if someone is damned, he must at one time have been a human being, but somehow he has forfeited his humanity and now he is floating loosely with the rest of the damned in no-man's-land. He hasn't a notion that anything might change. However it is possible to imagine a constant image of damnation. So only in the damned imagination can damnation exist as – conditional.

How can we make a picture of the human race? And what would that look like? Surely it would have to contain contradiction and opposition. Human race means warning and approval, means subjection and survival, breakthrough and abandonment, chaos and harmony. Finally then it means people and human beings. There the contradiction has become extreme and the opposition has become sublimely refined.

So one can say: The human race is our destiny. Our future resides in our origin. The reasonable mystery of our being here and now on earth may utterly embed itself in us because we are willing, as human beings – to be destined.[1] The true ethic is not a measuring stick that we adopt to pass the time or to torture one another but it evolves – within us. Our organic/biological origin is ethical, if we can bear it. So that we can bear it, we receive the word as gifted. I that not fortunate?

*

To come to awareness in order to avoid damnation – let us formulate it like that now. Coming to awareness means that we gradually become familiar with our human origin rather than living pointlessly day after day. The damned one, whose awareness has been stimulated suddenly, is able, on that account, to recognize himself as damned, and for that reason he attempts time and again to flee back into his unawareness. There, now, for the first time, he comes up against his condition of being split into outside and inside, and when he flees from awareness he can hide in only one of these – however then right away he is challenged from the other side. So he is assailed either internally or externally: internally there is error, there is insanity and externally there is delusion, there is mania. Both imply that one is challenged, assailed, because in truth one would be able to practice awareness, however one does not choose do so. So how can one help such a one to come to his senses?

First one has to understand he has not lost his senses; rather he has not yet come to them. Whether he is insane or manic, he has been stimulated to awareness and is therefore better off, in that sense, than the damned ones, who has not been creatively stimulated. If one sometimes now observes how damned ones undertake to heal the insane or the manic ones! Indescribable! Consequently the tremendous responsi-

---

[1] The triple meaning of the German 'geschickt', namely sent, destined (Geschick means destiny) and clever, cannot be reproduced in English.

bility of those who are adept at awareness. So much depends upon their works. Awareness is to become the norm and not remain the exception. It is also worth noting that those who resist what they experience as a challenge, an inner or an outer challenge, will not on that account become less insane or less manic, only their mania and their insanity will take on a more familiar appearance. When one now observes how those who resist these challenges try to heal the insane ones and the manic ones! Unbelievable! Again, all depends on the works of awareness. In terms of such works the afflicted ones may build themselves up.

*

Possibly the worst news is that those who do not understand their madness and their mania because they do not want to understand it or because they cannot, are no further away from their healed human being than those who consider themselves to be 'normal', having resisted the challenge of awareness.

Let us once more consider these three possibilities of being around or existing. While one is damned one is unworthy and one is unaware and ignorant of that. The concepts of insanity and mania cannot apply because the very sense is missing. Under damnation one is without sense, one is unaware and nonsensical, but not insane of manic. Now arrives the stimulation of awareness. One is pushed out, cast out, excommunicated from that 'comfortable', dammed existence and one is offered the opportunity of becoming aware. One is considered worthy and invited to be human. So for example does the Christ come into our existence here and now on earth and we only sense that we are damned, even while we are left at liberty to consider that as a state of the past. It depends now on whether we accept the invitation or not. That can take a long time. Often enough we are invited, for the one who invites us is merciful spirit itself. This state of being cast out[1] can in a trice turn into an awareness of having escaped and of freedom for us – if we so desire. It depends entirely upon our inward attitude and disposition, in other words on whether or not we work ourselves through to this human freedom that we are being offered. Not surprisingly the convenient old indolence draws us back. Damnation coaxes and tempts us – as shelter and security from awareness. A distorting backward glance confuses foolishness with a lack of cares. We certainly have worries and cares now, whereas before we had none.

Nonetheless as human beings we are considered worthy and for that reason this degree of progress is most important for us. Those who are not concerned about human dignity should not worry us. After all they themselves are not worried. However where the awareness is stimulated, there the concerns and the cares turn up too and we worry about our being here and now on earth, about our guilty past and our future under threat, about our questionable origin and about the premonition we have of our destiny.

Oh what indisputable proof of our human worthiness and dignity and of the fact that we are at liberty actually to come to true awareness are these sorrows and these cares!

Sorrow appears first – I mean the ontological sorrow itself, not yet a plurality of sorrows. How glad we should be, and what a sure basis he have for being exceedingly glad, as soon as the dark, still uncertain and undifferentiated sorrow arises in us and materializes before us like a fog! For surely it means that we are capable of healing awareness. And we should not want to be healed of that sorrow but of our being

---

[1] Rilke calls it: 'Ausgesetzt auf den Bergen des Herzens' in a late poem. (Exposed on the mountains of the heart)

21

damned, for it was no true being. As soon as we practice awareness now, the fog of that sorrow coincidentally clears up. 'Happy is he who sorrows!' What great wisdom is contained in this saying! He who chooses to become aware of this wisdom irresistibly grows into his human being – and sorrow always and again is proof for him that he can become more aware and it shows him in which direction to become aware. In the absence of this understanding, meditation and contemplation are useless.

Insane and manic then is everything that does not participate in this awareness when it might well do so, since it was worthily stimulated thereto. For whoever does not practice this awareness now, he automatically does the opposite, in that he longs to return to the condition of indifference and carelessness; he hankers for being without guilt and free of danger. He imagines a paradise, or a heavenly afterlife, which proves nothing more than that outwardly or inwardly, temporarily of futuristically, he believes in a salvation – which, however, in reality can only be available to him in his human being here and now.

Because he practices no awareness, when after all he could do that now, he flees into a schizoid hereafter – and is afflicted. This affliction means, not like sorrow, that you can practice awareness but rather that you are trying to avoid awareness and to flee from it. As a consequence you are divided in yourself. And now the sorrows, in their plurality, turn up too, where before there was only sorrow. This being challenged, assailed and afflicted – presents as mania and insanity. We ourselves are – our sense of ourselves is – challenged because we do not practice worthy awareness and instead we try to protect ourselves against the stimulation to awareness in our separate inner our outer state. It is insane or manic to attempt such a rescue. Mainly no such rescue is to be gained there – there is no such 'there' – and in addition the truth of the matter is that we are seeking to be rescued from the rescuer. That's crazy!

Let us right away be aware what this means. Just as the sorrow means that awareness is ready to be gained by us and that the worthy existence here and now on earth is available, so do insanity and madness, whichever afflicts us, mean that we do not need to be rescued but – that we already are rescued. If we were not yet rescued, from damnation, then we would succeed at this crazy escape-attempt, so that eventually we would be stuck again in our cheap comfort and our convenient popularity. That we do in fact not succeed, and that insanity and mania commence whenever we attempt this craziness, this simply means that thank goodness the realm of damnation is now locked for us and our return to there is made impossible.

If, however, we do not accept this meaning of mania and insanity, then once again we react, automatically, to the challenge, as though we were determined to have our crazy will and, in spite of the gate being bolted, we try to return to our damnation. That is somewhat more serious than our mistaking of our sorrow. One might call it satanic. The satanic spirit wants to persuade us that in spite of all signs to the contrary we still can – and should – 'save' ourselves into damnation. Those who are still damned and know nothing of budding awareness are more than glad to lend philistine support to this satanic attitude and sadly, for those who are insane and manic, the encouragement from the philistine camp to 'be normal' amounts to a siren call to the state of being actually damned and how can it help but horrify them. Sometimes, when the poor afflicted one, so to speak, senses in his flesh what it would mean for him if he really did return, such a satanic-philistine threat causes him, quick as a flash, to respond awarely and to dissimulate; in other words he pretends to be as normal as they expect him to be, if only he can gain some

23

time to practice awareness in peace. A true awakening may result then and there – or it can take years; decades.

The satanic spirit resists and opposes the challenge rather than understanding it. He who decides to get involved in this is insane or manic again, to a higher power. He dresses it up in all the latest progressive and modern technique and method, this satanic involvement. It even occurs out in the open, as Satanism or occultism. The challenge comes from two directions, so we can identify two sorts of satanic opposition.

*

The Satanic spirit:

In my own heart, in my own family, this satanic element is the most horrifying. So I have to ask myself: How can I forestall it? When this adversary appears in me, it takes a while before I am rehabilitated.

In any case I hope to ascertain that I myself do not become satanic, because then my humanity would be done for and I myself would have turned into a species of bad spirit and I would act and thinks merely to gain my own selfish advantages.

Not only in me but also in you do I hope to pre-empt this satanic spirit. What it depends on is my awareness. Not only do I want to act but also to *be* in such a way that this spirit cannot get a foothold in me. My awareness will then exclude the adversary specifically while I seek not my own advantage but yours.

Your wellbeing should be more important to me than my own. What sort of awareness is that? Is it even possible? After all my basic reason for this awareness is again, when all is said and done, my own wellbeing.

However a great deal depends on the goal I set myself. How I end up behaving towards you, that depends on whether I set my own wellbeing as my goal or yours. I have to begin somewhere and have no intention to remain stuck in my sensation – in my contemplation of things, so I set out to do something useful. This, after all, is an aspect of human being, that we cooperate with creation. My inborn human being drives me to do so. It is important for me to take this drive in earnest or I will make a mess of my life. Quite a few systems of thought and feeling exist in our cultural environment – some are religious – for which a bare contemplation suffices and in line with it one is to form principles according to which one is to act. This can sound most learned and clever and pious, however that central drive of my human being is not touched by it. I am supposed to squeeze it into the most diverse categories, while I know it to be greater and more embracing than the most sublime principles.

That I set my goal, first of my awareness and then also of my behaviour and action, outward of myself and in you, this 'suspends' that human drive, as drive, in me, so that I myself now am and behave and act in human fashion – no longer accessible to the satanic spirit.

Not you are my goal but my goal resides in you.

*

The one for whom bare contemplation suffices, we have said, abstracts principles from it according to which – others should behave. Entirely without action he cannot manage because even in him the human urge to cooperate with creation exists. So he thinks it necessary at least to pay lip-service to the need for action. He himself however does not act as he tells others they should and so his creative urge remains unsatisfied. He blames others and the world in general for that. He even believes that a God, whom he first imagines of course, has made it impossible for him to act, at least for now. So he burdens himself and makes his life miserable, mostly by deciding that he knows how others, including the world and God, should behave and act. "You must do like this and like that," he means, "and until you do, I cannot be a complete human being." His urge to be human remains compulsive because he only ever comes up with stillbirths.

What interests me here especially now is this urge or drive. Upon every instance of it, as it rises in me, I know that now I have the opportunity to cooperate creatively with creation. If I do not grasp it, I die and the drive continues to drive. If I do grasp it, however, and I participate creatively, the drive 'dies' and I gain eternal life – in other words truly human life. One is familiar with the saying: *His worm does not die*.[1] We become peevish, sullen, gloomy.[2] The human-natural drive nags at us if we do not creatively engage with it and it can even happen to us, if we wait long enough, that the satanic spirit becomes involved. We become habitually antagonistic. This is bad because now we can no longer help ourselves. Others must help us, those who know what is going on and we must at least refrain from contradicting them.

*

The human-natural drive – the satanic spirit – complete creative action: with those three we want to concern ourselves here. Whoever acts completely, and only he who does so, is immune to seduction by satanic spirit. So it is bound to matter to us that we know: What is complete action? For one thing, it involves awareness of what we call 'the messianic spirit'. We have touched on that when we explained how 'I

---

[1] Mark 9:44 in the Christian New Testament has it: 'Where their worm dies not and the fire is not quenched'

[2] A German might say: 'Es wurmt mich…' – it 'worms me'… that this or that is impossible.

see my goal in you' – no matter, by the way, whether you show me friendship or animosity. The main thing is – you are a human being. In the one who is human, who is stimulated to awareness as described earlier, in him I may, as a completely active human being, seek my goal and make it my intention. In that sense I may honour every human being because he is suitable and qualified, even whether he likes me or not, to be considered by me as a created being.

Each and every created being is human.[1] We can say: All that is is human. Of course not every being is a human being. This may turn out to be a difficult teaching while we think of human beings as somehow unnatural. We have, during the recent centuries, adopted the bad habit of talking about nature and human beings as if they were two different things. While human beings are things and nature is not human, we are bound to mistake men, women and children – who are human-natural beings.

So it matters now that we arrange these concepts properly so that words that have become current in some misconstrued form can be applied as realities.

All that is in reality is human. Being itself is 'humanly'. There is something like a human drive that is somehow determined in every creature. In us human beings this drive is to be determined that not only our being is human, as in the case of all that is, but that we become actual human beings. In terms of this thought all creatures align themselves again, gratefully in human being.

When we say 'man' we mean an abstraction and we do well to remain aware of that. Man is an invention, an heirloom, and a trifle. "Man is a giddy thing," says Benedick in *Much Ado about Nothing*, and who can say but he may mean

---

[1] Implied is the truth that humanity is the essence of being.

27

something similar. Not man, but human beings are to matter to us, and foremost those in our proximity, whose humanity we recognize and we honour them as men, women and children. Such human beings recognize and even understand one another: firstly as creatures, with an affinity to all creatures on account of their humanity, who show themselves as related to all creatures – and secondly as firstlings among creatures, to whom all creatures look up with good expectation and hope. Man as the crown of creation, that is an abstraction again, however it puts us in mind somehow of human beings as firstlings among creatures who, as men women and children, in honour care for all creatures.

One might say: Human beings, as creatures, are human once over again, to the second power. We are human, for we are creatures – which is to say we are. Beyond that we are human beings (if in truth we are that) inasmuch as that is what we intend to be, becoming aware and assured of our honourable position vis-à-vis all creatures.

However we must begin with other human beings. No one can honour beasts and despise human beings. As people, limited to our popularity, we diminish creation and turn everything around us into a wasteland. That is why first we ourselves have to become a wasteland before we can assert ourselves as creatures. In the meantime we stand below creatures, because we do not honour creation and do not participate in it, so that the human drive in us, the drive to be, is not fully suspended but instead it withers and atrophies.

Whoever points to another and says: 'You are not a human being,' or who says of another: 'He is not a human being,' betrays humanity, for that is the sort of thing people are liable to say, even when they 'commit crimes against humanity'.

*

We can see now how the satanic spirit may be utterly avoided. And only while we honour human being can we, without risk, make statements about that spirit. Under all other conditions we would not be able to avoid some involvement in it. The traditional saying makes sense: Speak of the devil and there he stands. Right away one notices too how this archetypal involvement always again creeps into our collective affairs because we are not yet sufficiently grounded in our human being as duty and privilege. Surely that is the very sun of our contemporary existence. Would we not do well to busy ourselves with our human being and our human becoming, since as people we can do nothing because we do not know what we do? The knowledge of our human being is the beginning of all our knowledge, for it shows us our relation with all creatures and – creates those relations at the same time. While we are modern we suppose we have to do everything so that anything at all comes into being. As contemporary beings however we can do whatever we wish because it already is. So we can see that this 'becoming human' depends on being human. Are you a human being? Then show yourself as one, and then you really are one. The difference between reality and truth becomes evident. What we are in truth, we may and can become in reality. This becoming consists principally in our works, so we should really not remain indifferent to how we can mutually agree in truth. The loving communion of all human beings brings our human being into the light so that we recognize and acknowledge one another as human beings. This acknowledgment is of first rate importance.

Where this acknowledgment is missing, the seed of the satanic already exists and we do well to become aware of that. This seed is then sowed as critical judgment. It practically happens on its own. The wind carries the seed to where it will find suitable soil.

*

29

Human acknowledgment:

In truth we are all human beings. And now comes a sentence that surprises even me: In beauty[1] people are human beings. This seed is good, and so, like all seed, it must die. Would that not be great, only imagine, if we as human beings were allowed to acknowledge people – on account of beauty?

We would better ask right away what kind of a thing such beauty is. It arose out of the abstract ideal, like Venus out of the waves, on account of the fact that we no longer speak of *the*, but of *a* beauty. Plato has arranged a few building blocks for this and we are grateful.

A beauty is a creature for which we can make ourselves responsible at this very moment. Precisely at a given moment we may succeed at this. So most appropriately vis-à-vis people this should work. And precisely vis-à-vis people we may behave in beauty and creatively – we may behave beautifully creative. This is not our way of keeping them at arm's length, no, that is not our goal, for that contains a critical judgment and a presumption. Human acknowledgement cannot arise while the satanic spirit has us entranced.

So for the purpose of human acknowledgment we do not necessarily need a human being in front of us; the possibility of human being suffices. After all we are not first to judge critically those with whom we will or will not have dealings. No, under the pressure of the still unhuman, a beauty spontaneously arises in me and becomes available outwardly. It happens because during that time I wish to exercise human acknowledgment. Where, in particular, the pressure of the unhuman originates or who is responsible for it, this does not concern me. I only wish to acknowledge humanity, actively and outwardly, even under that unhuman pressure, and there

---

[1] Beauty evidently conceived as 'the greater glory of god'.

30

then appears for me in the end 'a beauty' – a condition of beauty – as a creative work.

*

Human beings and people:

Only human beings, as men, women and children, are capable of creative human acknowledgment. Only they know how important such acknowledgment is, because their own creative human being is connected with it – and often it even depends on it.

So human acknowledgement is not defined by the fact that we acknowledge a human being as human and that we are, so to speak, aware of our human being. The acknowledgement is human simply because we ourselves are human and while we are human – and it affects every creature, in whatever condition. It extends itself over all that is, with knowledgeable understanding. One recognizes this attitude, for example, in those various surprising turns of attitude and behaviour of Jesus of Nazareth, whether he relates to future apostles or to present disciples, to Pharisees and scribes, to those who torture him, who condemn and kill him, even to a fig tree or to the satanic spirit itself.

By way of this acknowledgment one manages the connection to another being's valued being itself. That other being perhaps has no notion of the value of his being or of the fact that he himself *is* human. By acknowledging him we help him to become aware of it.

To treat people as though they were human beings – that would not be smart. Humanism, by comparison, is an attempt to understand all equally as human beings and is therefore a mistake. However, once again it should be carefully noted: One does not judge first and say: These are human beings and those are people, as if one could, from the standpoint of the

31

uninvolved or disengaged one, even recognize what is human. No, one knows of the difference between human beings and people, one is aware of one's own frequent less-than-human predispositions and tendencies, and one refuses to be long impressed by the mere appearance of things. Beyond that, one pays attention to circumstances, to how a situation unfolds and in general to what is happening.

*

Between human beings and people, each viewed separately in itself now, there exists an unbridgeable separation. No one may come from one side to the other. It is a matter of the dead and the living. No one can understand this if he himself has not experienced real and eternal life – which is to say if he himself has not been stimulated or motivated to human awareness. Human being and life belong together, and not only in our brain.

One may notice here how similar are the thoughts of rebirth and resurrection. People have to be reborn before they can be human; the dead must rise so that they can live again. As for resurrection, this means that we rise from among the dead, away from their influence, their conditions and affiliations, from all that still has no eternal life; it means that now we mean something quite different by life and that we undertake to realize this new insight, physically and organically. Previously we had capacities, intentions and reasons even as now, however now, from our present new-life point of view, we recognize, first hesitantly and then gladly (or first ruthlessly and then wisely) that previously these were all directed to a non-life. Gradually we distance ourselves increasingly from the negativity of that time, regardless of how positive it had seemed to us; what we are getting to know and understand now becomes more habitual. Once securely 'repatriated' in our new homeland we make a point of sending picture-postcards and invitations to those still struggling 'outside'. We do this invariably as individual persons and not as members of any group. Where we come to an understanding with one or two others in order to aim at the acquisition of this new life, there the measure of communal endeavour is already full to overflowing, as we soon realize to our amazement as soon as we come up with enough trust for such a breathtaking adventure.

To be reborn, in comparison to resurrection, this means that one is separated from people in order to be able to become aware of one's singularity and uniqueness, and so that one learns to bear the responsibility quite for oneself, active and suffering, and the passage to human being is narrow. We may take nothing along of our popularity or of our social dependencies and values. And once we have managed it, through all inclinations to lukewarm half-measures, through flights into sickness and insanity, through all silly habits and bad errors, then we may, in the end, even turn our attention to people, in case they should open their eyes and choose to see.

Our first duty, once we have arrived, is always to those who have been stimulated to awareness and so far they can barely help themselves. If once we have been introduced affectively to human being, we may well be like someone who hesitates in front of an open door and has no notion of how to take that first step. He who has an inkling of what real life might amount to, may well be the unhappiest human being of all only because he does not yet know his way around, perhaps because he has never before learned anything properly and because he has not the slightest notion of the myriad possibilities that exist for him, so that he may come into the possession of life and of more life – and live happily on earth.

* * *

Human Beings: Creatures and Gods

Whoever is familiar with human being knows he must be creative or else become less than human. Of course various ideas are current of what it means to be creative. One thinks especially of 'Art' and of being artistic. Perhaps one imagines 'Society' as a great organism that must be serviced like a machine. The artist serves inasmuch as he practices his art. Society admires and pays. The politician serves too, and the scientist, the churchman, the carpenter, the engineer, and the domestic maid. They all stand with one foot in their private life and with the other in public life. For all of them their existence is either private or public; however it is not always 'worthy'.

What is the connection between the business of art and creation in general? How is a housewife less or in some other way an artist than a poet? Has an author in essence a different right to be honoured by Society than a baker? And if someone stands in no kind of relation to Society, has he any right at all? And is that necessarily a disadvantage?

Being a human being means to be a creature, no doubt about that. It means more, but at least that. And all creatures are human, but not all are human beings. (Human beings are special cases – they are exemplary.) It may not suit us right away to hear that. In what way is a cat human? Surely that is nonsense. No, precisely not. A cat is human by dint of its being a creature. We have to acquaint ourselves with human being as general being. We have to think about it in such a way that we become aware of our relationship with all creatures. Stones, plants, animals. The sky full of light and clouds, the earth full of fire. The sun and all other heavenly bodies are human. What then is not human?

We ourselves, if we do not live creatively, are unhuman. Then all creation collapses in us like a house of cards.

Let us try to avoid abstractions, such as 'the' human being, 'the' animal, Society with a capital s. In the concrete, that is where we want to be at home. From the concrete point of view, as living beings that are growing and changing, we may discover our affinity to all else that exists. 'The' human being, as such, in Society, exists only as an idea. A human being, in comparison, is a reality. Let us prefer realities. Human beings exist as men, women and children here and now. All are creatively active; they do and they are done to; they act and they suffer – and this brings about the relation between human beings and all other creatures. In this sense we human beings are, for example, responsible for the relationships between all creatures that are not human beings, for only human beings can be creative. All other creatures therefore depend on human beings. Which is also the reason why there will always be at least some human beings.

*

A difficulty perhaps arises when we undertake to recognize human being in creatures. This recognition is not only the prerequisite for creation but at the same time its goal. Only logically looked at is this nonsense again. In reality I have this recognition and I look for it at the same time. I know that I have it and I search for it in order to own it. The important difference is between having and possessing. Between the two is where 'shaping'[1] comes in.

---

[1] I translate the German word Gestalt and its various derivatives as shape, shaping, shapely etc. This appears awkward at times, so I remind the reader of the connection to 'Gestalt.'

The goal of creation is the shaped recognition of human being in all creatures. Prerequirement for that is recognition itself.

Right away someone asks: 'How do you know that all creatures are human?' My answer is: 'What kind of an answer would persuade you? My father told me, would you believe that?' Or I say: 'Suddenly it occurred to me and when I acted accordingly, in other words when I went on shaping and giving shape, soon certainty arrived. Does that make sense to you? Or I might say: 'It was given to me. It is 'a given', the way some philosophers mean that, and now I give it to you. Will you accept it?' 'Not necessarily.' 'Aha, you want me to show you how to do it. But I am just now doing that. This written text you are looking at, it is humanly exemplary and it is a creations, including creatures.'

Do we wonder about the difference between creation and creature? What human beings come up with creatively, those are creations and they are endowed with human being. Our language, English as such, for example, is a creation and human being adheres to it. Since it adheres to it, it can also be loosed from it. This present text is a creation, because the prerequirement for it, its end or goal, is the recognition of human being in all creations.

Human being that adheres to all creations is something very special. It is valuable and precious. The 'binding and the loosing' of it has to be learned. This is part of our being human as such.

*

The humanity of all creatures – that is the archetype of what is true. And human being that is bound to all creation – that is a very special feature of us as human beings.

36

Our creation – what it means to us and what it should mean to us – with that we want to busy ourselves for the present moment.

We humans are creatures, true enough, and we need to be aware of that, however among creatures we are a special case. One consideration is the main point: We succeed in leaving our home and we return to it. What our home is, that can be discussed. Not much depends on the name. *The* human being, the abstract-ideal human being – does he at all have a home? No, he looks for it. He hasn't a notion where to look, the poor chap, and he doesn't know where he belongs. He has no place where he can lay his head. For that reason we pity him and we want to help him. We as human beings have a home, which we can cheerfully leave and to which we can joyfully return.

Creation, imagined or not imagined, is our home. In creation we are at home. Creatively we leave it and creatively we return to it.

What does this mean now: creation? It means the bond of all creatures. Homeland for us human beings is the bond of all creatures. That all creatures are human, that binds them, and that is the origin of the bond.

Why does a human being cut himself off from this bond? Does he suddenly stop being a creature? Not that, but we know now of the difference between having and owning. We know how we hardly feel secure within ourselves for very long before we want to prove ourselves as human beings again. It is not enough for us just to exist as creatures. Not that we stop existing but that we also want to exist creatively. So we leave your home and loose ourselves from the bond of all creatures.

The creature that looses itself from the bond of all creatures and returns again in order to bind itself with all creatures – that is every human being that gives evidence of himself as human, by being creative.[1] For that reason too do all other creatures depend on him. In the absence of creative human beings, creation would fizzle out. By this we do not mean to say that such a danger can ever really exist, but we emphasize the sheer necessity of human beings. No need to worry that the supply will ever run out. However we can consider whether we would prefer fewer or more human beings around us, and so we are reminded of our ambition and of our timidity. Timidly we draw back into our existence as creatures and gradually we become less human. Then too, we are no longer creatures but we are among those who perish and those who are lost, who all get together anxiously in fear of the day of judgment when all that is useless is strewed like ash unto water.

Ambitiously however we put ourselves to the work of creation and we leave our home, so that we can express our concern for human beings and for more human beings, in order to bring them home and to show them exemplary human existence.

*

So human beings either exist creatively or else they lose their human being. And the quintessence of 'home' is itself understood as the bond of all creatures, which we leave creatively and to which we return; time and again, not only once. He who does not leave his home does not know it as his

---

[1] At this point, reader, why not read Rilke's wonderful poem that begins: "Taube die draußen war…"

home, and so he has none.[1] However he who chooses to care for other human beings, gladly leaves home, for their sake, and he abides for a time, for their sake, in his own creation. During the time of his abidance he proves himself especially and in exemplary fashion as a human being. He reveals human being and renders it accessible.

Nothing really and truly compares to human being, which is simultaneously abstract/ideal and concrete, which is no less corporeal than spiritual, and which we may know as what is most precious in the world. The essence of being is humanity. It allows itself to be handled and grasped. Visibly it exists and invisibly it endures. We cannot get around it and without it we cannot get on.

Human being reveals itself to us and becomes accessible to us while we are creatively active, which is to say active and suffering. No one can show us how this is done; each has to find out for himself.

*

Creative activity exemplifies human being in the light of day and human being cannot be divided. It is atomic.[2] What is beautiful about that is that we do not have to wait until someone allows us to have this substance or until conditions are just right. I can help myself any time. Do we realize what that means? In the morning, at noon, in the evening, at night we can help ourselves to that substance, which could be called the true nourishment of human beings.[3] There is no

---

[1] Consider TS Eliott's apt reference to this: "We shall not cease from exploration, and the end of all our exploring will be to arrive where we started and know the place for the first time."
[2] Only consider how man's search for the atom, for atomic power and weaponry, merely simulates his search for his true human being.
[3] Why not take a quick look at John 4:32 in the Christian Bible, for comparison.

getting around it, as a human being I am highly privileged. Precisely that which strengthens me, essentially, as a human being, is at any time available to me. I only need to want [1] it and I have it. I have something now to which I can direct my entire 'wanting', and no chance of disappointment or uncertainty. I believe I am more than content with this, because my wanting has always again gone astray in the undergrowth of a million possibilities and time and again it has miscarried in pursuit of the imagined life, so that I came close to flight into optimism or pessimism. Now I know exactly what I want and it should never again happen to me that I lose my direction so that I have to backtrack.

In order to make this clearer and more comprehensible, let me add at this point that along with the wanting, a certain amount of daring is required. I dare to want human being. We should think of it as a boldness, not as a casual convenience or a half-hearted sideline. We might even perceive a risk – however we want it nonetheless.

So at the start we want it in spite of any and every convenience to the contrary. It can happen that the desire for convenience and complacency turns up as soon as we demonstrate that we want this food. Now we do well not to negate or to suppress this desire because it does guard us against any inordinate willing. Perhaps we have a tendency to become

---

[1] Throughout this text I translate the German 'wollen' in the sense of 'to want' but also in the sense of 'to long for'. 'Wanting' implies both that we miss something, that we 'have a want', and that we express the wish to have it. When we ask someone: 'What do you want?' we should always to and extent perhaps mean: 'What are you missing?' with the implication that we might well be able and willing to help him get it. The expression 'to long for something' emphasizes that what is not appropriate here is 'willing' in the sense of 'insisting on our right', of the 'satanic' willing as we come across, for example, in Goethe's *Faust*: "Du mußt! Du mußt! Und kostet es mein Leben."

immoderate or exorbitant in our willing, and by that we would spoil our chances at getting what we want here. No, simply in spite of, or better said – in the presence of – this desire for convenience do we choose to want and do we long – and now we are surprised how this inclination to pleasant circumstances and feelings turns into satisfaction and gratification. This then accompanies us as we want – and receive – human being.

*

This precious substance corresponds – *with* our wanting of it. We do not say here 'the wanting', as we might say 'the human being', but we speak of our wanting. And surely we can want or not. And in the absence of something that we want we cannot want. Of course we might 'have a want' but now we know what to want in order to satisfy that want. So without intelligently wanting something we cannot really want. We can test that in fact we want and that we actually do want. We do intend to be aware of the fact that we 'want' and not to do it blindly. Do you long for comfort and convenience? That is a kind of wanting but human being does not correspond to it. The human being we want fits each and every one of us truly and completely. To want human being, this truly satisfies our human nature. Cosiness, congeniality, even sociability – these just do not qualify as goals for what we truly want here. We are not created in that way, that we should above all else want it easy and leisurely. If we do, contrary to our nature, set these conveniences as our goal, why then we achieve the exact opposite, which is only just right, otherwise would we not falsify and spoil our nature? Also – whoever would spoil all these pleasant conveniences for someone, he is like the one who beats the servants because they are not masters. Of course we are tempted at times to aim at what is pleasant and nice, but whoever resists this temptation sinks even more deeply into it.[1] When we are stuck in quicksand we must remain still until someone throws us a plank or a rope. The perfect response to this temptation – both to the temptation to prioritize pleasantness and niceness and the temptation to resist or suppress these, whether in ourselves or in others – is simply our wanting of, our longing for, human being instead.

Some have more difficulties with what is unpleasant and others with what is pleasant. If we diligently long for human being, neither of these will burden us. Mind you, this specifically diligent longing is mainly suitable for those times when we are burdened by life. Diligently we carry the load, then our life is no longer burdensome, but then diligence becomes pointless, because after all we want human being once the burden is gladly born. We still want human being, please.

The 'wanting nonetheless' changes the burden into affection and the longing for what is pleasant into satisfaction.

*

It is pointless to prescribe for anyone what he should want but at the same time surely everyone would be well advised to long for human being. What does it look like? Useless question! As you are at this moment. Surely the way you are changes all the time. You cannot pinpoint it. So long for human being, regardless of any appearance.

Then it becomes part of your creativity, because you are being creative, are you not? That makes a difference. You work and you are effective. That should all be creative. In all of it human being should become apparent – this human being that you want and for which you long. Your efforts are pointless unless they are informed by human being. We talk

---

[1] Let the ascetic beware!

42

in all sorts of ways about labour and work, about what is made and done, but unless the purpose of it is to bring human being out into the open, ahead of all else in the world, then it is a waste of time.

With creation as 'all creatures joined by human being' we are familiar. What, however, is *a* creation? Who can say that just at this present moment he is being creative and not wasting his time? Or how does one ever begin, since we always continue with the next creation?

Something has to serve, so that human being comes into being, that it takes on shape (Gestalt). It does not allow itself to be transposed or transported shapelessly; that is after all the whole point of human being, that it, so to speak, fills out the spaces between creatures and mainly between human beings.

So we furnish ourselves with some stuff, some material, so that human being as the carrier will become known. A creation may consist of stuff and carrier, where human being is the carrier. While I am creative I am, throughout the process, conscious or aware of the difference between the material and the carrier, however from the point of view of the shape or gestalt, no such difference can be ascertainable.

Now if someone wishes to be creative for his own sake, specifically to recreate himself, he only wants human being and takes no interest in any material or stuff, so any difference between the two does not signify. He comes into the possession of human being for the simple reason that he wants and longs for it. If, however, he wishes to be creatively active, he reaches for some matter (which is then his material) in order to achieve a work, a creation. If he undertakes a creative work, he intends to give shape to human being. If he makes use of a creation, he has decided that he himself wants to be creatively active, which is to say to do and to undergo, to act and to suffer.

One may notice that this looks quite different from what one commonly imagines when one speaks of artist and public, of a product and the pleasure in the enjoyment of it.

*

Human being allows itself to be bound or loosed. Any creative activity always turns our regard to itself. As a creature I should remain secure in my bond with, my relation to, other creatures but time and again I miss out because I do not 'want human being'. I neglect to long for it. To long for human being, that means to be creatively active. My longing definitely desires to develop in that direction. And the stuff, the matter I employ so as to be able to shape human being – the origin of that should remain indifferent to me. Human being, we might say, seeks it out for itself. [1] I myself then bind, where stuff and carrier, burden and bearer, fit together. I bind in that I do what is required to set it up and set it out ('hinstellen' and 'hinausstellen'), which is to say I shape it (gestalten). I realize it for myself, such as during a personal learning exercise, or I realize it in the light of day, available for others.[2] The revelation of human being is the main task, and this is what interests us here. Human being shall no longer be concealed but revealed; that, after all, is what we want and long for, and what moves and motivates us. Revealed human being is our final goal, is the end of our hu-

---

[1] Can we in fact depend on the human being within us to direct us to the particular matter that would be most suitable for its realization? Undoubtedly. In fact our good works depend on it. Some will say they create out of nothing when they mean to imply that human being, after all, is invisible and cannot be imagined or pictured. All the same, if we hope to enlist elemental energy, upon which truly good works depend, we must take humanity as such into account.

[2] I see no reason why the German *Gestalt* and *gestalten* should not be translated as *a reality*, which has been verified, inwardly, or *realized*, outwardly. Always, by the way, there are those two possibilities for us.

man history. Our creative activity, and productivity, always again issues into this end-state, this final condition, where we are human among human beings, not merely human among creatures, and not merely creatures among creatures. The latter will not endure in any case. Being human among creatures we can bear for a while, but then we have to decide, do we want to be creatively active or lose our human being again. Being human among human beings, which of course implies being human among all creatures, we will always again be renewed, for our substance increases and is increased. Simultaneously human being is revealed in the world – as world.

What we call world here is the end-condition of world-history, is the here and now of eternally live reality. World is the world transubstantiated. Revealed human being is materially present as world. And the stuff? That is what the world was, dissolved in itself and newly bound. The end of the world is – world. We know that the world is in dissolution and from there we derive our stuff and material whenever we realize (gestalten) human being, so that it is revealed, as world. We are the human beings then who return to their home and – all is different. We recognize ourselves now as creatures and our creator, who realizes us, we simply call god. We recognize ourselves not only as creatures, which is to say as creations of this creator but also as human beings among human beings, in world, who are themselves creatively active, like god, and consequently we are called gods. We suffer one another as god suffers us and we love one another as god loves us, For that reason we are called gods. We are creatively active, like god. God works, and we also work. God reveals himself to us and we reveal human being – for him. Those who understand this know eternal bliss and blessedness.

*

45

What we call human being, that is substance, that is carrier. As gods we are entirely borne by human being. In every human being a contradiction surfaces when we speak like this of human beings as gods. This contradiction has the effect of a loathing, a disgust or aversion on our psychic half-being. Resentfully the repulsion leaps out of us and behaves destructively. That is the resentment, the aversion, the unwillingness which energizes and supports, and then even brings into the light of day the psychic 'half-being' (*Halbwesen*) – as monstrous.

Nonetheless we human beings stand as gods before time, and our own being desires that we reveal and assert ourselves as such, creatively active and suffering. It is precisely this element of suffering that is so unacceptable to the psychic half-being. It cannot accommodate itself to it and has to become chaotic – to degenerate and get out of control. Then it confronts us as monstrous. This confrontation is characteristic. Scenically and sensationally it suddenly stands there and 'acts as if'. This means it gives itself out as not a half-being but in a way pretentiously demanding and arrogant. One also gets to know it as a horror and as an energy that demands its own rights.

A god recognizes it as a half-measure and rebukes it, purely by means of his worthy being. A god is revealed human being embodied as carrier. Carrier of what? As carrier of material that allows it to appear as 'in shape', as reality (Gestalt). The effect that Jesus of Nazareth had, as a god, on his environment, as described in the Gospels, becomes, in this sense, more understandable. The creative spirit he emitted lured the bad spirits our of concealment so that they made themselves known. Bad spirits destroyed themselves when confronted by this god. Today we may find ourselves in the company of psychic half-beings, which we might define as bound bad spirits. In other words they are not yet destroyed –

but distraught, unhinged. This perturbation hangs around the necks of us human beings nowadays like a chain of the sins of our ancestors. It is transported over the generations, this fetter, and the magical claptrap of the modern world lends it a delusory perpetuity.

What is missing is the confrontation of the monstrosity by gods. Where the appalled psychic half-being manufactures its appalling disturbances in the light of day, there divine spirit must assert itself entirely without resentment, and we succeed at this if we allow ourselves to be borne entirely by human being – which is to say: in that we are gods.

In aid of definition: He who is a human being is not necessarily for that reason yet a god. We become gods at that moment when we intentionally, and in order to destroy and negate the psychic abomination, rely entirely on human being as our bearer: which means that we ourselves become the material that makes it possible for human being to appear in the light of day as it confronts that which is appalling and horrifying. As gods we not only want complete human being, but we ourselves become shaped human beings (Menschengestalt). One does not accustom oneself to that but one allows oneself to be edified and elevated. A god draws us up to himself. This is well known but not often thoroughly understood.

To want, to long for, human being completely – that in itself stirs up the distracted spirits and brings them to the light of day. A human being sees them and knows them right away and does not allow himself to be terrified by them – which he manages if he becomes entirely material, which is to say pure being-here and quite without will. The turn-around is noticeable. One is willing to be human up to the threshold of the appearance of the contrary will and then one lets oneself get carried by one's human being. One steps into the foaming water of the stream and then draws up one's legs. The god swims stream-downwards towards the ocean.

Whoever allows himself entirely to be borne by human being– to be sure in order to help others to become human, to be a shaper of humans – allows himself to be not only creature but also creation. We allow for that at the moment when we decide not to contradict or resist the abominably contradictory will of the terrifying psychic half-being. We let the monster rage until it ceases – until it has spent itself. We are mainly passionate now – and without a will of our own.

*

Human beings are creatures. Gods are creations. A human being is a creature of god. A god is a creation of god.

The disgusting thing, the horrible and monstrous thing, is unhuman and evil. It appears while we long for human being. It shows itself precisely because we want human being, because it cannot bear the pressure of what is good. It has to present itself to us.

As soon as we want human being we are with god on the same path, because god wants human being. Would it make much sense to long for human being if it just lay about? No, everywhere we look, in ourselves or externally, human being sweats and strains under the drudgery of the unhuman and barely knows how to help itself. How can good advice be useful in that case? Human being cannot will itself, so how might good advice be useful? The will to human being, that, after all, is human being itself, and if that is missing, and where it is missing, there inhumanity sits in the judgment seat and arrogates. It does this for so long until it is confronted by a will to human being – by a longing to be human – and then it is outraged and makes a terrific scene. Then it unmasks itself and appears as the counter-will and shows itself to be the monster that it in reality is. At that moment we see it separate from the human being it had subjugated. On account of our will to human being we have loosed human being from the inhumanity, so that now this inhumanity appears to us as loose. That which is visible is loosed and the invisible human being is also loosed. That which is loosed on earth is also loosed in heaven – if we may express it in this traditional sense. Heaven means invisible, earth means what is visible.

And now this boastful strong one, this evil inhuman one who has come out into the open, is to be bound, so that he can no longer assault the human one. So we lay aside our will and allow ourselves to be borne up by human being, of which we know. The contrary one now cannot find anything in us against which he can strengthen or maintain him- or herself and so he is bound, so that he can no longer budge. At the same time we allow ourselves to be borne by the loosed human one, of which we are aware, and we successfully bind ourselves with him. Now he is bound too, in the sense that he will not again be lost. So what is bound on earth is then also bound in heaven. Not that this traditional manner of description elucidates what we mean, but that we understand this saying better now – that is our reason for referring to it. We do not nowadays differentiate like then between the visible and the invisible realm, between earth and heaven, between being and essence. And the contemporary doctrine of this difference has not yet become current. We can however take note that the facts which result from the action that has been described above manifest the visible and the invisible realm as, so to speak, two aspects or points of view of the same reality. What we call reality and the human world is equally visible or invisible, depending on whether we know it or believe it. And what we call the realm is the kingdom of heaven on earth. And all that is, also has an essence, for the essence of being is humanity.

*

Allowing ourselves to be borne, or carried, by human being, i.e. becoming entirely stuff: might there be other ways of explaining that? We are stuff when we do not want or long for anything. We interrupt, intentionally turn off, our longing, so that our human being, of which we know, can become shape. As stuff and carrier the shape 'takes place'. If human being is the carrier and I am the burden, then human being shapes itself as I. I let that happen, in awareness of my goal.

Does a god then still have an identity? Does a god say of himself: I am in order to be here and now? And in what sense is a god also a human being, since he has stopped wanting to be human?

Well, we are not human beings because we want to be human but because we have human being. For that reason are gods also human beings, because they have human being. The substance which we call human being belongs to them too. When a human being becomes a god he does not forfeit his substance. On the contrary, he makes something out of it. Better said, he allows himself to be made out of it. The human being which previously was being wanted – now it works, is effective, on its own. We do not say: the human being which the god previously wanted – because previously he was not. Previous is not possible for a god. In that sense, very likely, Jesus is reported to have said something like: "Before Abraham was, I am." And that a human being does not stop being a human being once he is a god, that is implied by the fact that this god still owns the being that is human, even though now it also works and is effective in him.

As a god you are, however you are not this or that. Being this or that is connected with wanting and longing. Identity, on the other hand pertains to this and that kind of being. To my question: 'Who are you?' a god replies: 'The human be-

50

ing who is speaking to you.' After all you are not for nothing a god when you are a god, but you are a god in order to be a complete human being. If people call you a god then this should not please or irritate you, but when you are with people, quietly be the human being you are, because then human being is effective in you in a way that cannot be overestimated. Nor can it, in fact, be estimated at all, strictly speaking, because when you are a god, god works and is effective through you. This effect is then such as it could not at that moment be any better, for it is truly good. Not you are good but the effect which god has, or wields, by means of your 'Gestalt'.

You know that this effect is certainly good. What more do you want? You may contemplate this effect and you notice: it is simple and sufficient. The visual aspect of it is not sensational, is certainly not charismatic, is not persuasive. In its simplicity it points you to what is on the way for you, prospective, as future, and definitely as 'in shape' (gestaltet), so that destiny leaves you in peace. That which is sufficient about the effect reaches back to the past and – blesses it. It 'calls it good'. You might say that you thrive in history.

*

Being stuff oneself and not wanting or longing for anything while letting oneself be borne up by human being so that a shape can come about – this allows itself to be described as being a god. Complete human being stands before us and is effective. Such a 'Gestalt' is not ideal but bodily. The ideal withdraws from before it. Which is also why all idealism has to step back from what has taken shape in contemporary fashion. It has, so to speak, to make place for it. In this time we live today and will continue to live. A god, and every god, is our contemporary – which is what god 'wants'.

51

Do we get along well enough with what has been shaped (gestaltet')? This is worth thinking about, in the absence of signs, since no shape is outstanding or distinguished by a sign. Consequently neither vanity nor jealousy can get a hold on us.

So let us consider now this one 'Gestalt'. Stuff and carrier determine it and turn it into what it is. All that is spirit and flesh but not just one or the other is body. Being human and being stuff is embodied as one, is palpable. We do not select any stuff, but we allow ourselves to be carried, as stuff, by all that drives and weaves, within and without us, which is everywhere. 'Gestalt' is therefore not a concept but a word and as a word it presents itself to all drives and it weaves in exemplary fashion. All that is human, within and around us, of which we know and for which we constantly care, does after all want to become material (stofflich = stuffly) so that it may show and prove itself in the light of day. As destiny and history it wants to manifest and to testify, and that is our human-natural intention then too.

*

Human being in the light of day manifests itself as 'bearing', namely as carrying and suffering. The Gestalt to which we pay attention is not found in being but in becoming. There no thing may be differentiated from another. The borne stuff is manifest solely in order to make the bearer, that human being, palpable, and this we an feel like a trace that we may follow. This feeling, this trace, leads us directly into that which is human such as we can all make use of and as each one of us can use. The stuff embodied with the carrier facilitates and simplifies for us our approach to human being. Embodied stuff does not remain attached to our individuality; in me as person, in you as person, it evanesces; it enters into and becomes entrance. Then that which is human has embodied itself in us.

The stuff that shapes me and the stuff I shape; the I and the you merge into one another. However what it all depends on is the human being, not the stuff, not the material, which melts away and vanishes – after it has had its use, being used up now. Not outside of us, not inside of us but simultaneously a shaped human being appears and steps into us. It does not force itself upon us but it appears suddenly – where we could not have expected it. Also there is no protection against it. Object-subject, private-public, absolute-relative, all this collapses in that shape – when that shape 'is the case'. And with that we naturally mean the one Gestalt.

Only one thing is useful, and that is the material or stuff that was incorporated into us and that merges into us in the meanwhile. And in the same manner do we manage with our own creations, which we 'set out' so that others may shape themselves ('sich gestalten') in terms of them. We are not missing anything, nor do we have to wait until we are sufficiently formed or informed. Our creations flow out from us like a stream – we experience and feel it like that. That is again the same trace we mentioned earlier. On paper or in whatever matter, this trace can be experientially followed, so that anyone can settle into it to his benefit – if he so chooses. However then, in the end, he first and last has to want and to long for. *No one can do himself good in terms of our creations unless he 'wants' physical and organic human being.*

*

We have to make a point of shaping human being, otherwise we will not get ahead. That which comes, futuristically and that which has passed – destiny and history – all make us new as human beings. Even as it suddenly dawns on you, namely that you know and understand, the good news pre-

53

sents itself to you, in fact and in the wink of an eye, and softly upon the feet of time, which smoothly glide over all that is inconvenient, you may prepare yourself for the most crucial event of all – of which only a few inform themselves, a few who are proudly in possession of a truth and who manage to guide everything around them merely by way of always gladly overcoming and cheerfully suffering, in spite of a backlog of fear and of a burden of incurred guilt.

He who does not honour human being, for him his existence is agony and affliction – or a half-hearted indifference. Life and death for him are equally mere gestures and rumours. One lends oneself to the nonsense of the modern world and to the evils of one's unknown heart until in the end there is total collapse. Surely that should suffice! However the race for success exhausts us: we cannot know the time. Improvements are available. Now and again something good works out for us. Under the influence of creation we may confide in one another and eventually the miracle happens in which we then live – while the 'powers and principalities' haplessly disport themselves as on clouds.

* * *